SHE LOVES ME NOT

SHE LOVES ME NOT

self love poetry
with & without words

TORI DOYLE

DOYLE

She Loves Me Not | Copyright © 2021 by TORI DOYLE

All rights reserved. No part of this book may be reproduced in any manner whatsoever without written permission except in the case of brief quotations embodied in critical articles and reviews.

First Printing, 2021
Illustrations and cover design by Tori Doyle
ISBN: 9780646830544

A catalogue record for this work is available from the National Library of Australia

www.torigdoyle.com.au

"for all inner children that need healing"

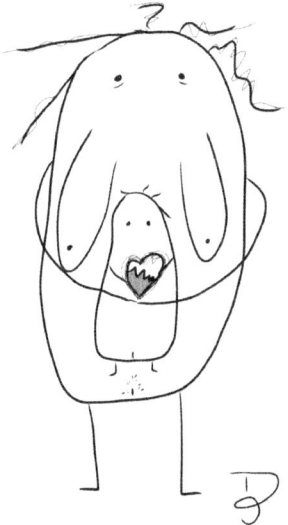

-about the book

"She Loves Me Not" is a collection of self love poetry.

Take a journey through these five stages of healing, as depicted by one woman's inner child, as she navigates to become a woman of love & purpose.

o Nurture
o Explore
o Accept
o Personal Power
o Love & Connection

You the reader can explore all five journey stages, allowing you to add your thoughts and reflections in the "she loves me notes" at the end of this book.

Tori has unapologetically written from a visual perspective of a "dyslexian", free verse and free in interpretation, with and without words.

-about the illustrations

Illustrations in this book have been drawn by Tori Doyle and represent an expression of each poem. Tori uses art to express how she sees emotion, "writing without words". Her tribute to all those with learning challenges.

The female characters in this book are all called Daisy, she is the centre of her world. She comes in all shapes and from all walks of life, beliefs, values, and shares a common thread, which is to heal, love and connect. She is perfect, because she is one of one, she cannot compare to any other.

She is beautiful, strong, resilient, and okay not to be okay some days. She picks out her own thoughts, just like picking Daisy's petals.
"She loves me today, tomorrow she may not".

CONTENTS

nurture 1

explore 45

accept 89

personal power 119

love & connection 153

nurture

go back and nurture yourself
let your inner child rest

-she loves me not

she loves me not

guilt
hurt
worthlessness
resentment
abandoned
unappreciated
overwhelmed
depressed

                                                      she loves me

                                                      freedom
                                                     wholeness
                                                        worthy
                                                     forgiving
                                                 supported
                                           appreciated
                                                      peace
                                                        joy

                                          she loves me today
                                       tomorrow she may not

-her

you speak
    i listen
you hurt
    i suffer

  her a girl
  me a woman
  her my shadow
  me my enemy

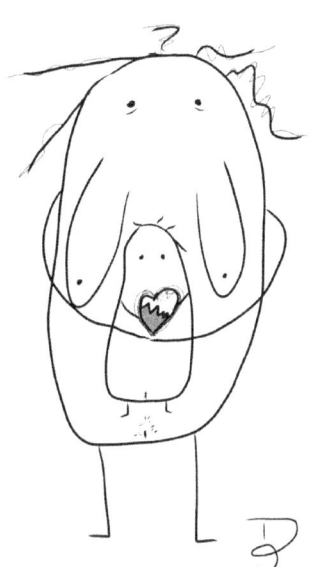

-the gift

fleshy gravel
caresses my fingertips
a keepsake gifted
never to be returned

fingers dipping in
    dipping out

of the man made ridge
restores the memory
of the gift passed down

    breath stops
        restores the present

fleshy gravel
caresses my fingertips
a keepsake gifted

never to be returned
    never to be regifted

talk kinder to yourself
            you might like it

-broken

she is not ready to encounter
the force of life

unable to bloom

broken away from the stem
too late to strengthen her core

too weak

she shrinks without water
leaving behind a faint trace

of the beautiful bud she *was*

-born

born with a stigma *born from a girl*
born with lies *born to rebirth*
born with new skin
naked
untorn
she is born

-mask

her inner child
suffers

she creates a mask
    to hide her pain

-her trauma

she asked me
   how would i describe it

i said there are no words
   just feelings

find love in the deepest part of you
nurture it

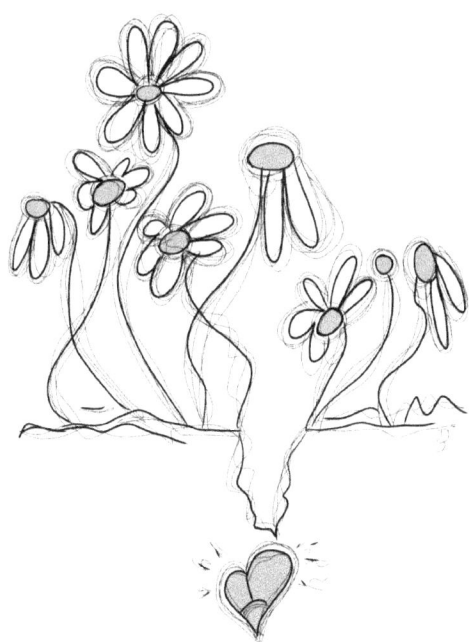

don't let your thoughts
    fuck your day up

                                                            -rice

i will never understand
you trying to bring me down
i will never understand
why you wanted my power

didn't you have enough

i will forgive myself
for not understanding me
i will see you just as
a grain of rice in my life

    small

       i will never let you
        define me

-inner child

in a bunker
she waits

metal helmet on
she waits
gun in one hand with clenched fist
she waits

breath shallow refusing to rest
she waits

cuts on her skin unable to scar
she waits
head noise silencing her voice
she waits

exhausted
she waits
on guard
she waits

in a bunker
a woman me

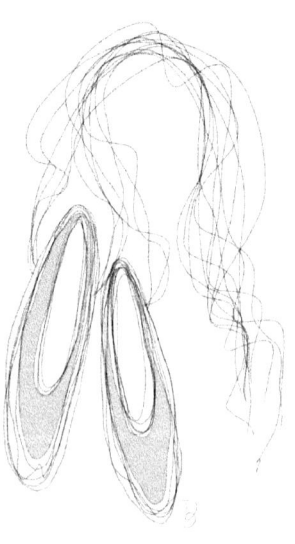

-ballerina dream

a perfect point barely touches the floor
her arm extends to the grace of her hand
her ballerina's dream whispers

r e a d y
now she waits

her breath is warm
her bed unsafe
her pirouette takes flight
she leaps in
her body still
her mind's dream takes her to dance
until her body is released from cold hands

she unties her shoes

hangs them at the end of her bed
ready to place on her bruised feet again

-let go

her cheeks blow up
her hands are cupped
her heaviness
she can't keep up

releasing you
she's let go

her heart now lightened up
this toxic load

-special

special
a beautiful thing to be

with marks on her thigh
and a special pain
left behind

-honour her

she needed
to *heal*
to *stop*
and honour her
    this inner child

-mamma

can you hear me walk away from you
    when i hear you slam your door
do you see me outside smiling
    as i am talking to the birds

do you see me when i run and hide
    to a calm and quiet space
do you hear me whisper *i love you*
    at your door when I hear you cry

can you hear me when i'm singing
    to a song you've sung before
if only you had sung with me
    the fighting may have gone

can you feel me when i'm laughing
    at your favourite tv show
i see the tension in your face
    the sadness in your eyes

how come you can't see
    how much it's hurting me
how can you just not know
    why can't you feel my presence
my heart is begging you to
p l e a s e
love yourself enough
so you can love me

-gone

rusted old swing
my old friend

you lasted through
my childhood

you may be gone
but i live with the memories
of the comfort you gave

the *songs*
the *tears*
the *laughter*
the *conversations*

you were my safe place

    thank you
    my only friend xo

my inner child
she is in here *tangled*

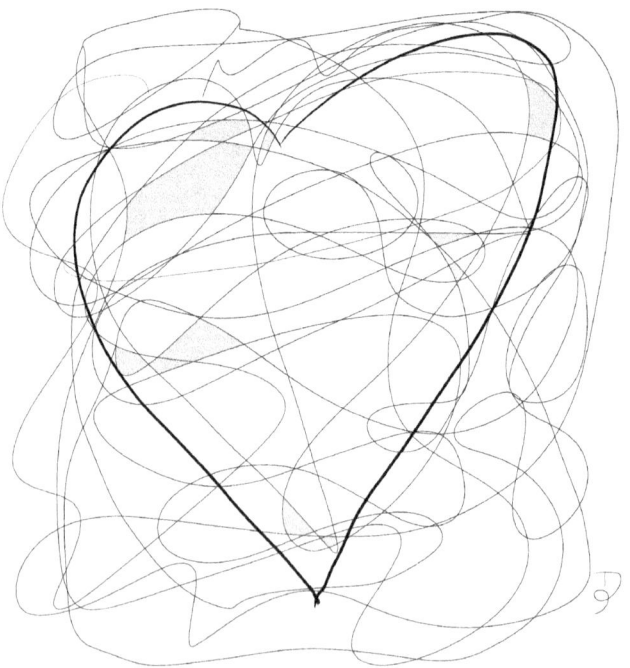

-safe

she is my child now
i will cherish her
    heal her
    love her
    honour her
    she is now safe in me

-waiting room

i think about them
when i rub my hand down
the back of my leg

i sit

triggered

i see my reflection
in the mirrored letters
of the waiting room

empty

-hurt hurt

why do you pick out faults in me
you know
they are not imperfections i see

there are no parts
just *w h o l e n e s s*
of a beautiful woman in front of me

are you so hurt that you can't see
the power of words diminish

self esteem

are you so hurt that you can't see
you are a beautiful hurt

just like me

-radio

transistor radio
sits in the grass
carefully placed
between a rug
and her ball

it speaks
in wandering song
pushing against
the sounds of trotting hooves
as he moves the dial

song disappears

back into the grass
no longer calm

    no longer song

-ingrained

her ingrained feelings of *hurt*

she nurtured it

it was then she felt
her heart respond

-awake

her inner child awakens
ready to suckle the bosom
of the woman she became

a *nurturer*
a *protector*
a mother

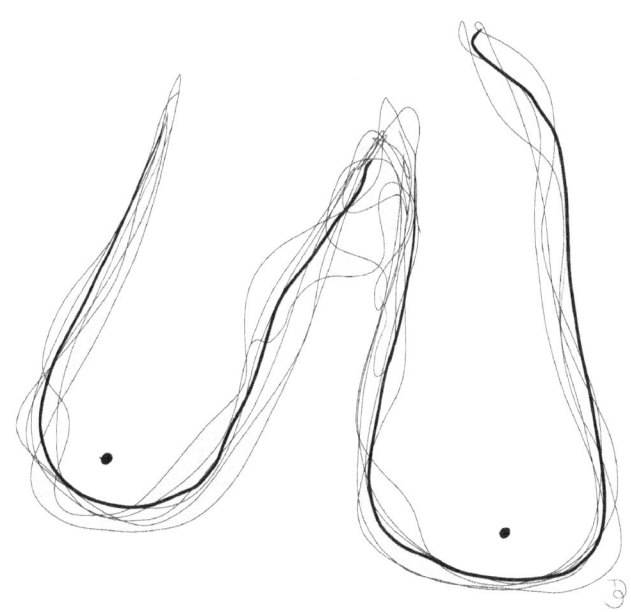

-stupid girl

stupid
is the word that sat in her gut
nails pointing out
scratching at her confidence

just like she remembered
how it felt that day
when her teacher
dug her nails in
    squeezed around her heart

the lesson she was teaching
wasn't understood
she took to screaming out demands
to read this grade three book

this lesson was not wasted
resilience is what she learnt
she pulled out every nail
of how she should be taught
and every single judgment

    is nailed to the floor

explore

her thoughts awake *ready to explore*

-you say

you say
you want trust

you say
you want respect

you say
you want honesty

you say
you want kindness

          you say

-bloody chair

this bloody chair
her comfort space
waiting for it
to finally break

this bloody chair
holds her weight
of all her judgments
and mistakes

this bloody chair
it remembers her
each time she sits
sinking into
her permanent dip

this bloody chair

-courage

she takes a step on courage
where clarity she'll find

it will be the light in search
of her truest form to shine

leaving all her ugly thoughts
instinctively her duty

and show the world just herself
with all her innate beauty

she'll be a beacon of self love
a guiding beam to step on

and as we stand together
a new strength is formed

taking this new courage
and watch our lives reform

one of self acceptance
    and resilience has been b o r n

-her moment

she stepped out
for a moment
to feel and breathe
this air

in this
her moment
is her time to explore
her own self care

-journey

she is here where she needs to be
where her feet stand strong
at her crossing

where her hands clasp at the front of her chest
holding her space
she's ready for change

she faces the sun to revive her energy
nature's warmth floods through her eyes
where she needs to see

her heart expands out
feels the pull of her call
that she hears ahead

    she takes a b r e a t h

takes her step on this new path
that she accepts

    this journey is her

-crestfallen

crestfallen

her hand reaches out to anyone
who understands *her worth*

        her spine breaks

her hand withdraws

when she doesn't understand
her worth *herself*

o p e n
closed

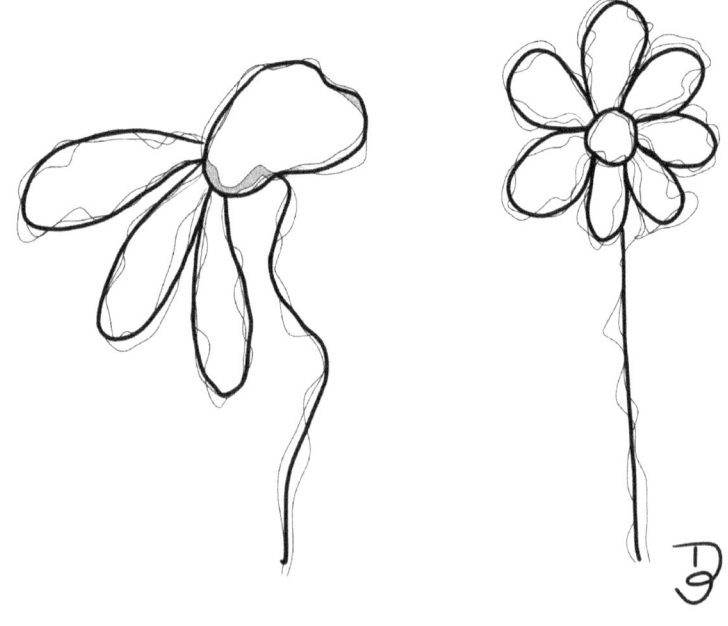

-two versions

her words she cannot speak
there's no meaning in them
they're worthless
so weak

how can she love herself
when all she has is doubt

her worth
her thoughts
her pain

too shameful to come out
she shows herself in pictures
who she pretends to be
she knows it just an illusion

of who she should really be

-explore

my gifts and talents are unsure
i have this time to explore

be it less or be it more

there is always time
    to self explore

i can see a future me
it's time to stop procrastinating

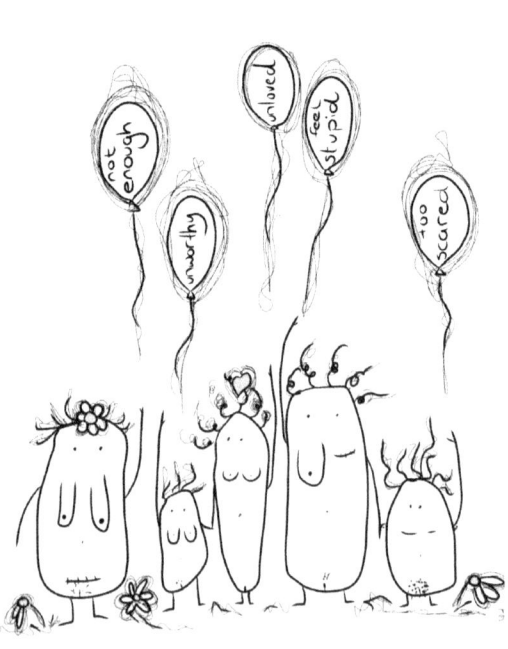

let go of limitations
    you'll find your passion

-daisy are you okay

daisy
are you okay
you were stood on today
your stem and petals all dismayed
your delicate life has been maimed
  will you ever be the same

i am a daisy
this is true
i might look delicate to you
just look around me
you will see
that all these daisies
  have been stood on too

-choose

my faith is damaged
my trust undone
this dark winter had no sun

my feelings numb
as i come to see
nowhere to go
when there's nowhere to be

left alone
i now call home
in my head
there is a tiny space
to dream the dream
of a brighter place

no magic key
to unlock these gates
only the keeper

will choose my escape

-gold

not what she has
not the power she holds

what she does
is her self worth
g o l d

-no room

my mind is swollen
a scalpel needed to take this swelling away

no room for hope
when shame and guilt clog this sacred space

no room for hope when i'm blind to see
finding space is what i need

is my life worth this fight

>*is it hope*
>or is self love the key

-without

without the darkness
there is no l i g h t

without self love
there is no f i g h t

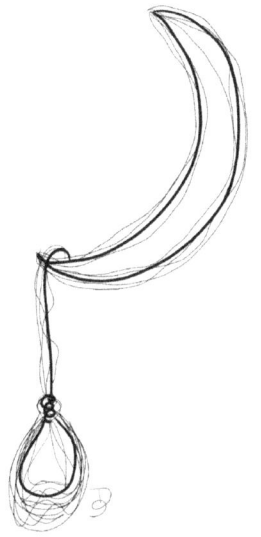

-listen

you will hear me say
i want to run away

you'll hear me say

you will hear me say
i'll find love one day

you'll hear me say

you will hear me say
i'll just fade away

you'll hear me say

you will hear me say
i'm okay

you'll hear me say

you will hear me say
thank you today

because you heard me say

-her & i

she hears the sound of her heart
    i hear the sound of mine
out of beat
but still okay to move her feet

she feels the touch of her soul
    i feel the touch of mine
so different but still entwined

she hears my voice in her head
    i hear hers in mine
two different things being said

    only one   o u t s h i n e s

                                                              -just for fun

just for fun
let's say *she's done*
just for fun

let's say she's done with self hate
what then

will she see her *beauty*
will she feel her *calm*
will she hear her *breath*
will she awaken new *thoughts*

so let's say just for fun
she's done

-aim

she aimed for perfection
and hit her flaws
as she did
  she became confident

-in my head

i tilt my head
it won't come out
these thoughts i have
that people said

i am worthless
not enough
to be the girl that can love

these thoughts i live with
now for good

who are they

these people i don't know
or is it me
that this i said
then i should be the one to

    remove this from my head

-bang bang game

i shot myself with my own thoughts
of an ugly picture of me in shorts
this picture came to play
with everything else i hated that same way

if only this picture did not exist
i hate the way i surrender to it
my self esteem *i deeply miss*

b a n g   b a n g

too many days with me on the ground
picking out bullets i had found
time to change this *b a n g   b a n g* game
i strike a match
light this flame

hear the sound of disservice thoughts
burning through to my souls port
and underneath these ashes i see
my self esteem here
still with me

accept

she accepted herself
then everything changed

-i accept

i can accept
my story

i can accept
the present

i can accept
my past will never ever *change*

and because of this
i can accept the woman *i became*

-same

paper plane
paper crane

add a flame
they burn the same

she accepts all of the woman she is
loved & confident

-unchanged

a familiar breeze that enters the trees
she has felt

familiar trees that dance in the breeze
she has seen

a familiar sigh when she watches this dance
she has breathed

a familiar feeling that stays unchanged
she has been

-stay

where is she running to

she just accepted she's here to stay
being present
enjoying her days

-sing

i sing

i dance

i love

i pray

that i can love me more
even in these fucked up days

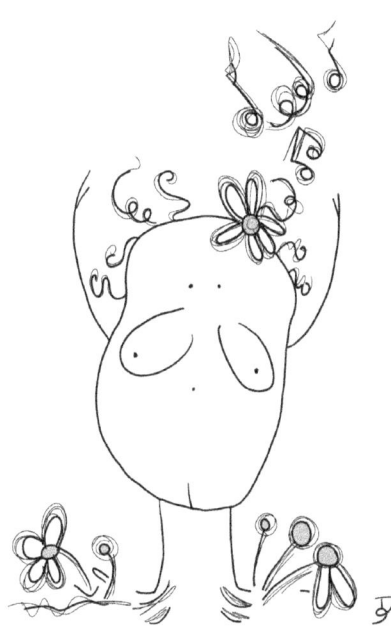

-reflection

she laughs
her world is laughing

she feels joy
her world is joyful

she cries
her world is crying

she lies
her world is lying

she explores
her world is the adventure

she loves
her world is loving

her reflection she sees in her world she believes
    her world is her reflection of her beauty to see

-gave away

she gave away her sorrys
to the ones she blamed
accepting what is becomes her natural shame

too innocent to recognise this fire has just started
will burn through her worth
until this woman has departed

she gave away her sorrys
to be faithful to her shame
holding on to guilt is her burning flame
accepting that this is who she chose to be
her whole life deceptive unchanged

    she'll see

lying in the ashes of self hate
she saw no way out *no escape*
her ear to the ground
feels the vibration of sound
her heart beating fast
she *whispers*
    s o r r y
        the last

-chasing love

she tried to catch it since she was young
chasing love from everyone
out of breath *she's holding on*
the love she holds is just too strong

slips through the cracks it shies away
her chase no longer for love to stay
she changes direction to lust she claims
she knows it just a woman's game

to have this pleasure
to hide her pain

over time her truth awakes
that love is something you cannot take
she sees it in her woman face
for the first time feels
her self love faith

she no longer chases love to stay
her love is her *in every way*
now her tears pass her lips
she caught this love
    this feeling missed

-liberate

she accepted *their* choices
    she became *suffocated*

she accepted *her* choices
    she became *l i b e r a t e d*

the search for validation
stops here

-still this girl

her
laughter

her
light

her
silly self

her
cheerful smile

her
witty style

i touch the lines on my face
i'm still this girl
make no mistake

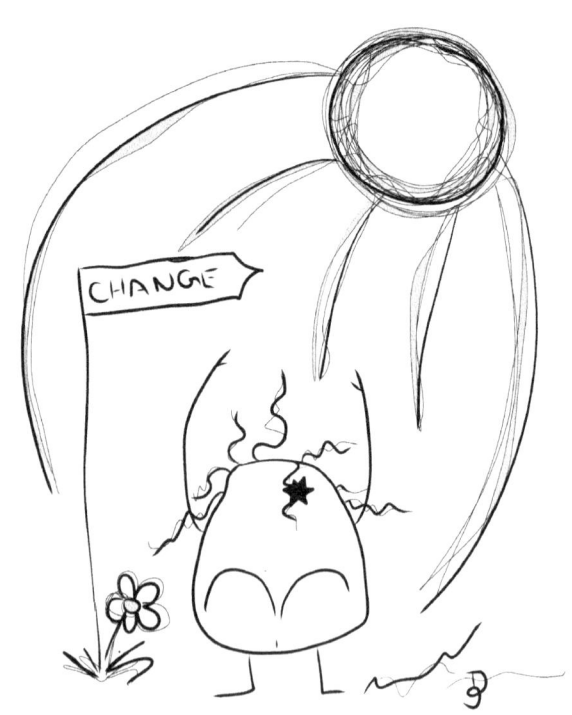

-change the game

they said who cares what i look like
it's what's inside that matters

i say
i'm not beautiful
my life broken
sharp shards
entirely shattered

how can i love this body
with its scars and pain

years of my own hate
my body shame

for me to love this body
i need to change my game

commanding any confidence
to power up this brain

dissolving my self hatred
     of any *unloved claim*

-if only

she is strong
if only she knew how
    strong she is

she is confident
if only she knew how
    others see *how confident she is*

she is loved
if only she knew how
    much she is loved

she belongs
if only she knew how
    much she means to the world

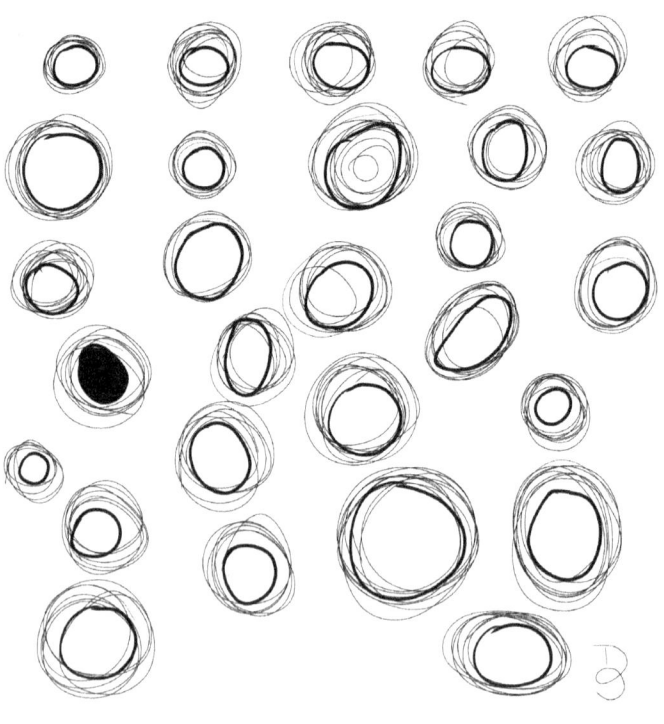

-look

hey girl
look at who you are

one of one

you can't compare
you with any other

you are perfect

just as every other

personal power

take back your personal power
stop giving it away

-colour of me

look closely through
earths blues and greens
through the cracks you'll see
a flicker of yellow not wanting to be seen

it hides it's life
underneath the colours that belong
invisible and stepped upon
if stayed too long

it's vulnerability is exposed turns grey
this little flicker becomes small prey
lying l i f e l e s s on earths floor

a new warmth is explored
golden rays come shining down
a new emerging insight found

earths yellow becomes the brightest light
even in its darkest night

y e l l o w is the colour that was me
    g o l d is now what i choose to be

-i am enough

i am strong enough
to crush harsh words

i am loved enough
to make them fake

i am smart enough
to shake them off

i am kind enough
to love myself

i am enough
to now stand free

my belief is enough for me

-harvest

to cease tradition she's not a fool
of bygone women *their repetitious rule*
her heart is open she rips the seams
unites her hopes and all her dreams

she takes these seeds from which she's torn
from this gift *a harvest born*
nothing more to bestow
just her naked body

    content and free to grow

-my power

i love to wear high heels
and my sex appeal

i embrace my woman traits
the way it makes me feel

i love my powered self
this feeling of complete

i love the fact i get to choose
    what to give and what to keep

-glassed

our words collide
shatters you inside
with a flick of your wrist
you've thrown glass into this

blood on my lips
this taste is exposed
how was i to know
you need to heal and grow

how you react
    you're in charge of that

so i'll take a step back
not to tread on the glass
tip toe back onto
my own path
leaving your words
to be the *last*

-plugged in

self love is power
when plugged in

connecting you
    just step in

-the coat

she was a fool to wear this coat
an obligation placed upon her
a tradition that serves to tell the story
of who she'll be

like the women who wore this coat before
pledging their life *submissive and contained*
these threads heavy and insane

her duty now has shifted to a selfish thought
this coat will no longer offer its passive thread
instead

she lifts it off her soul
removes it from her timeline
abandoning it in history

never again to hold

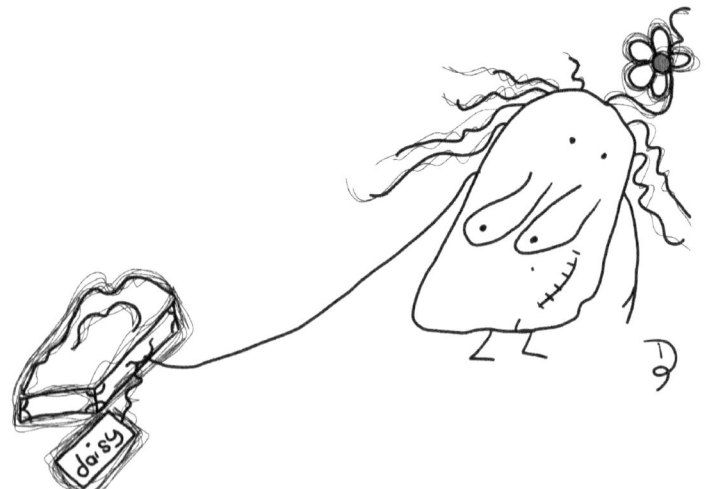

-baggage

she drags her feet
her life incomplete
holding onto *baggage*

her life's work

of seasoned thoughts
and self worth damage

so heavy now

her confidence lags
time to pull off these tiresome tags
she cuts these ties

says goodbye

leaves this baggage far behind
she walks ahead feeling light
sees her newfound confidence is

in sight

-i define me

i define me to be
an empowered woman
i see in front of me

she demands her destiny
lives with honesty and integrity

a colourful she
wears and looks as she please
reflects the love she is to be

doing the best she can with dignity
being defeated gracefully

a woman standing her ground
pushing through her trauma or disability
her limitations *she does not see*

in between her hearts pulse is an interrupted echo
from the impotence of others defining her to be

but i always hear her
    w h i s p e r
    i define me

-whispers

don't mess with my mind
i became strong

don't close my heart
i became open

don't ignore me
i became heard

step away from my ears
your whispers unclear

go back to the past
    i became u n m a s k e d

-echoes

do i look fat in these
do i look okay
is anyone going to stare and say
what the hell is she wearing today

it's funny that it's just not me
that questions this each day
it echoes through the world
in many different ways

time to stop this message
we're not the women that we say
time to raise our voices
and tell the world we're perfect
in all our different ways

let's celebrate our choices
and praise that we have gained
an understanding of
every woman's pain
for acceptance
to be the same

take a moment and look around you
its not just you that said
every other women has the same
questions in her head

time to put an end to
this old choice *i'm not enough*
replacing it with *i am fucking fabulous*

a new echo is said

-her drum

she is

crazy
funny
smart

she beats to
her own heart

-queen

yellow all grown up
    now turned *g o l d*
   she transformed

-astronaut girl

this astronaut girl ready to fly
holding her papers and astronaut guide
excited to leave her childhood behind
she heads for the stars *ready to shine*

on her way up with transforming worth
the atmosphere turns she falls back to earth
awakens her being to an unwelcome goal
her astronaut life left deep in her soul

this astronaut girl met an unvarnished truth
her quest had changed from the one from her youth
with instructions within she creates her new mould
adjusting her role *her coordinates unfold*

leading to a place ready to explore
this girl's new life too big to ignore
her purpose is bigger than what she first thought
her papers unqualified for this astronaut

her heart will guide her for this new flight
when her wings open up and let in the light

this astronaut girl has fallen away
only her truth stands strong enough to stay
raising her head her quest she shall not fear
the sun has risen yet the moon still near

she sees the whole picture it's suddenly clear
a remarkable woman she *shines* standing here
she raises her hand and touches a star
and remembers there's no need to *fly so far*

-fish bait

yesterday i was timid and shy
today *i will rise*

yesterday i was unsure and unwise
today *my courage i will find*

yesterday i felt unsafe and small
today *i stand in awe of my power i explored*

yesterday i wanted love and just wait
today *i will no longer be fish bait*

I waited patiently
> *to become the hero of my story*

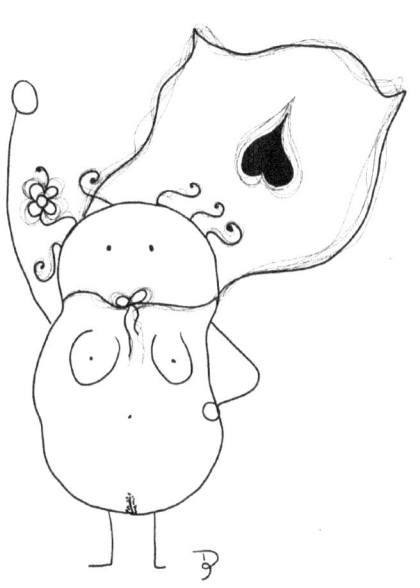

-permission slip

i give myself this permission slip
to love myself from here on in
and have my life begin

i give myself permission
to accept all of me
accepting all my parts
to feel the fullness in my heart

i give myself permission
to stop sabotaging my life
this one i am deserving of
and all my greatest love

i give myself permission
to let go of all the hurt
to stop punishing
what i thought my life was worth

i give myself permission
to trust and to be free
to live my life that i intended
right before i stopped *believing in me*

love & connection

she connected to herself
that's when she fell in love

-daisy chain

i stand alone in a field of daisies
watching them sway together when strong winds blow
raising their song louder as white birds fly low

small   old   tall   young
every daisy here *belongs*

their hearts whisper with the beats conducting on
i nudge further in to hear them *s i n g*
finding myself wanting this life of mine to begin

i took a step back on the path i just left
discovered loneliness was my gift to bring
no song or love no treasure to be
all i had was just me

the winds grew stronger and for them to stand
they all held each other with a strength they all share
together they come as one with a faith
in the eye of a storm when all hold each other
they are beautiful
    o r n a t e

i stand alone in this field of daisies
but alone i am no more
my place is here
a sacred space is cleared

i join their song
i now belong in a chain of daisies
feminine and s t r o n g

-i you we

i matter to me
you matter to you
      we matter together

i forgive me
you forgive you
      we forgive together

i love me
 you love you
      we love together

i belong to me
you belong to you
      we belong together

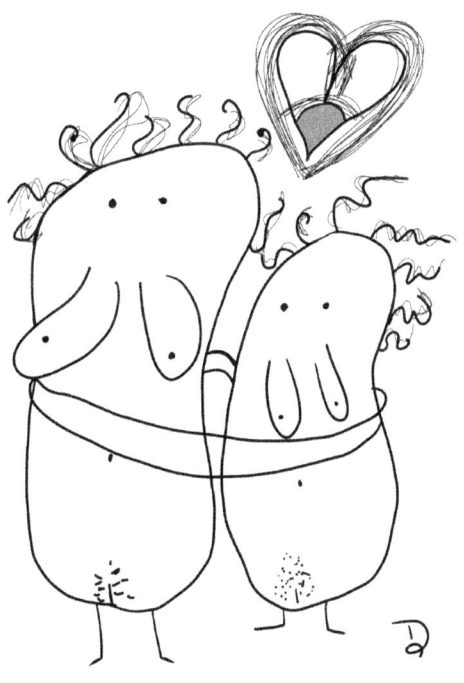

␣␣␣␣␣␣␣␣␣␣␣␣␣␣␣␣␣␣␣␣␣␣␣␣␣␣-no fear

she caught the connection
it flowed around her heart

she asks
what did i do to deserve this love

this question showed no fear or anxiety
just love

-it's me

i love
the way i look

i love
the way i sound

i love
the way i feel

i love
the way i think

i love
that the person that loves me the most *is me*

-gypsy

roaming like a gypsy
    no home for me

i can only see
what's in front of me
a world of my own fantasy
of sunset breezes
    of desirability

living in my world
    of freedom to be

being a gypsy is for me
not stuck in a time zone
    to dilute thee

i belong to just me
nothing else i see
will ever change
    the gypsy in me

-i see you

just this once do you see me
before i unravel and fall

just this once can you lift me up
without taking score

> *can i count on you*

when i am feeling lost
or will my neediness come at a cost

> *do you see me*

as i see you
a friend that understands

to have a friend is an honour
and not sold on demands put upon her

-lifelines

i run my fingers over
the lines drawn on my skin
each one a mark of life
that was ready to *begin*

i feel these hollow dips
these marks of life i see
then look over at this tiny face
this life i grew in *me*

these lines i am so proud of
this is my truth to see
these are my lifelines
and what they *mean to me*

-dear ten year old self

how do i start
when i know how others left their mark
i'm sorry

when i tell you to be brave
please listen
a woman you'll become
your body will awake
your resilience and inner strength you'll take

your courage will be your mover
into your personal power
to lift you up and stand alone
in your crucial hour

this is all you need to know
this is what will help you heal and grow

so just wait
this life you live is not the same
new love for life is what you'll gain

you'll see the change as your self love grows
this woman you become reflects and flows

and as you read this new love awaits
your life is yours to navigate

so hold on tight
you'll be alright
you know your life is worth the fight

i'll be here waiting when you've come through
and hold you close to me
i am the one who understands
this life of love you need

and when you're in my arms
your safe and out of harm

ready for the next adventure
beautiful and calm

love me xoxo

-rebirth

i close my eyes and meditate
walking into my safe place

my seaside haven
my comfort space

i feel the air brush through my hair
as though it was still there

i dip my toes into the sea
my heart opens with calm and ease

i smell the ocean mist
i feel it on my lips
this kiss of life i'll forever miss

my heart is full

i say goodbye to the life i had with you
i take a breath
rebirth awakes

    my life is now with *g r a t i t u d e*

-bubble

life's little bubble growing within
can you feel the love seeping in
now in two *i overlap you*

watching you mimic life to be
you'll never be alone in this life you see
connected are we

i'm holding your heart
while you create who you are
the joy i feel
when you find your path

trust your soul
to the journey you become
i am a mother
we will stay as one

my love for you will never end
now we stand side by side
mother and daughter soul friends

sharing the love when i touch your hand
    watching your own little bubble expand

-glows

reflect and flow
is when a woman grows

love and connect
is when a woman glows

the end came first

the beginning came next

-she loves me notes

self expression opens your mind to new possibilities

i welcome you to explore your own journey to

- nurture
- explore
- accept
- find your personal power
- self love & connect

i hope your journey leads you towards a life you can only imagine.

tori xoxo

-i nurture notes

-i nurture notes

-i explore notes

-i explore notes

-i accept notes

-i accept notes

-my personal power notes

-my personal power notes

-i love & connect notes

-i love & connect notes

-notes

-notes

-acknowledgements

This book would not have been possible without my own experiences, and the love and support of my family through my exploration into my own self love.

I owe an enormous debt of gratitude to those who helped and inspired me along the way. Brittni Davies, Kai Jacobs and Nikki Roberts for giving their time freely to assist with clarity, insights, and encouragement to produce this book in my own diverse way of writing, with and without words.

I appreciate my family's support, my two children and their partners, giving me the strength to put myself and my story our there to help others.

Finally, I want to thank my husband George, for his love and understanding, and for making this journey with me worthwhile.

-about the author

Tori Doyle is a poet, artist, and art therapist Adv.dip.tat, working with women and children, helping them navigate life.

Tori writes from her own life experiences, drawing on her resilience and courage whilst embracing her gift of dyslexia. She believes that poetry can be healing, and she uses it to inspire and empower women.

When Tori is not writing she can be found sketching, and enjoying time with her family. She has also been seen chilling in nature and dipping hers toes in the water, with an afternoon cocktail.

She currently lives in Queensland, with her husband and two cats, Theodore and Happy, one calm and the other a little energetic, a bit like Tori herself.

If you want to know more about Tori's next books, please visit her website at www.torigdoyle.com.au where you can sign up to receive updates for new releases.

www.ingramcontent.com/pod-product-compliance
Lightning Source LLC
Chambersburg PA
CBHW070253010526
44107CB00056B/2447